Rivers and Lakes

by Imelda and Robert Updegraff

Published by The Children's Book Company, P.O. Box 113, Mankato, Minnesota 56001.

ISBN: 0-89813-043-3
[Previously assigned ISBN: 0-416-88140-8]

This edition is for sale only in the United States and its dependencies excluding the Philippine Islands.

First published by Methuen Children's Books Ltd., 11 New Fetter Lane, London EC4P 4EE

The Children's Book Company
Mankato, Minnesota

Contents

Our Mighty Rivers

The rivers that cross our earth like long flowing ribbons of water are very important to the people, plants and animals which live on the land. Rivers drain unneeded water from the land. They also change the landscape by wearing away the rocks and soil and washing them down to the sea.

Hundreds of years ago, almost all our towns and cities were built beside rivers. This was because rivers were the best source of fresh water for people and animals to drink. People also found that the land beside a river was good for growing food because the soil was rich and wet.

The land along the Nile River in Egypt has been farmed for six thousand years. Every year the Nile floods over its banks leaving behind a huge area of wet fertile soil, excellent for growing crops. The Ancient Egyptians learned how to divert the river water across to the land. This kept their crops watered even during the dry seasons. This is called *irrigation,* and it is still used all over the world to make rich green land out of the deserts.

Long ago, when roads were poor, rivers were often the best means of travel. The Mississippi River was important in this way to the early settlers in the United States. The riverboats which steamed up and down this huge river were sometimes the only link with the next town, or even the outside world. The riverboats were also the only way the heavy bales of cotton could be carried from plantations to the mills in the big cities. If you look at a map which shows the Mississippi or the River Rhine in Germany you can see how many large cities are linked by these important rivers.

In the 1800's people who lived along the Mississippi River far from big cities were very glad to see the steamboats arrive.

Rivers are always on the move carrying water across the land. They carve and change the earth, wearing it away and carrying the soil down to the sea. This is known as *erosion.* The kind of path a river makes depends on what kind of land it flows through. Rivers can carve through solid rock to make deep canyons with steep walls, or wear away softer surfaces to create wide valleys. Stones, sand and soil are washed down by rivers. They are piled up at the mouth of large rivers in broad flat layers. These are called layers of *sediment.*

Water falls on the earth in different forms. It comes as rain in the summer and sleet or snow in the winter. Water is stored in the damp soil and held in lakes. It is locked up in snow on mountains and frozen in the ice of *glaciers.* Rivers are made up of water from all these sources. They collect the different kinds of water together and carry them down off the land. This keeps the earth from becoming a giant swamp.

Mountains divide the landscape into different regions. The rain which falls on the north side of a mountain can end up as part of a river hundreds of miles away from the rain which falls on the south side. These separate areas of land are called *drainage basins.* They can cover small areas or stretch over whole continents depending on the landscape.

Most rivers begin as small streams high in the mountains and far from the sea

Drainage Basins

Rivers drain water off the land. A drainage basin is the area of land which feeds a river with water. The basin collects and stores water from rain and snow. It soaks up the water like a giant sponge so that the earth is kept moist for plants to grow in. The extra water is passed on to the rivers. A drainage basin includes rocky ground high in mountains and the dark rich soil of the plains. The size of a river depends on how big its drainage basin is and how much water falls into the basin.

The mighty Amazon River in South America has a huge drainage basin containing millions of square miles of tropical rain forest. As this is an area some forty times the size of England, it is not surprising that the Amazon is a much bigger river than the Mississippi.

Not all the rain that falls on the land runs into a river. Some evaporates back into the air, and some is drawn up by plants. The rest soaks down through the soil where it is stored in the earth. This is called *groundwater,* and it trickles down through the ground to lower levels where it comes out as springs of cool fresh water. Rivers are kept flowing in between

This cut-away view of the land beside a river shows how the groundwater can not sink down through the layers of clay and rock and keeps the river full.

rainfalls by these underground springs which slowly release water which has been collecting. Water can also be stored in lakes or as snow on mountain peaks.

As the water in drainage basins eventually comes down to the rivers, it is very important that we are careful with it. Rivers must be looked after so that their water is not wasted in times of drought. It would be very hard to live without rivers which give us water to drink and irrigate our crops. It is also important that rivers do not get too full and flood the land they run through.

Most important of all, the water in drainage basins must be kept clean. If chemicals from factories find their way into the soil, even high in the hills, they may be washed down by the groundwater to the rivers below. This may kill all the plants and animals that live in a river and could poison the water so that it remains undrinkable for years!

Our Amazing World . . .

The Amazon River in South America is the largest river in the world. Its flow is greater than all the waters of the Mississippi in the United States, the Nile in Egypt and the Yangtze in China. Its mouth is 110 miles wide.

Rivers

Rivers wind and flow across the land in many different ways, but they are always moving down. They are looking for the easiest way to carry their water to the sea, and often change direction as they flow.

Waterfalls are rivers taking the shortest way down. They are found in rocky regions and mostly in the mountains. Waterfalls are sometimes made when the river suddenly changes direction so that it runs over a cliff or other steep drop in the landscape. They can also be made by a river flowing across deposits of soft rock which is worn away by the plunging water.

Rapids are also found in rocky regions. The rock is so hard that the river can not carve a deep channel through it. The river has to flow very quickly as it pours across its shallow rocky bed. This makes the water froth and bubble. Many towns were established along rivers next to waterfalls and rapids. It was either too dangerous or impossible to go farther up the river in a boat, so people and cargo were unloaded to continue their journey by road. Towns grew larger as they became important stopping places on well travelled routes.

Tributaries are smaller rivers which run into bigger ones. A tributary collects water from its own drainage basin which is usually far inland and distant from the sea. When a tributary joins a main river, the two combine to make a larger river.

The flood plains are areas of rich, flat land below the mountains. The land is rich because it is thick with soil and minerals washed down from the heights above. This soil is also very moist because the water does not drain off the flat land so quickly. Floods often happen in the spring when normal rainfall is increased by water from snow melting on mountain tops or during periods of heavy rain.

A delta is sometimes formed at the end of a river. It is made of soft fine sediment which the river has brought down from the land. The water loses all its force when it reaches the sea. It drops the soil it has carried as the river slowly merges with the vast ocean.

The sediment in a delta is washed down from the mountains by the tremendous force of the rushing water. This wearing-away of the land is called *erosion.* It makes dramatic changes in the landscape which can take thousands of years to build up or happen suddenly overnight.

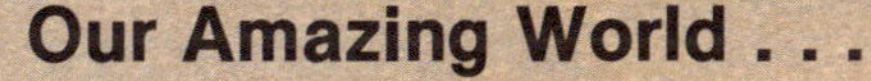

Our Amazing World . . .

Niagara Falls in the United States is the largest waterfall in the world. 1,600,000 gallons of water pour over its edge every second, and fall down at the speed of 50 m/p/h. The roaring water cuts through 3 feet of solid rock every year.

flood plains

Erosion

The land around us is always changing, but this usually happens slowly over millions of years. The high mountains which are pushed up by the earth's shifting crust are steadily worn down by the action of wind and water. This is called *erosion.* If new mountains were not being made, the earth would finally be worn down to a huge plain, only a few inches above sea level, by these powerful forces.

Rivers start high in the mountains, sometimes several thousand feet above sea level. The force of the water fiercely rushing down from the heights is the most powerful form of erosion on earth. It not only wears away the land, it also carries the worn-away material such as rocks, sand and soil, down to the sea.

Some of the mountains on the earth such as the Himalayas, the Alps and the Andes have only been there for a few million years. These tall craggy mountains have steep-sided valleys and small areas of plain. In time, their shape will be completely changed by erosion. The mountains will be worn down to rolling hills, the valleys will be wide and most of the lowlands will be broad plains.

Some of the effects of erosion do not take so long to be seen. They can happen in the space of a few years. In times of flooding, or when rivers are running fast, the features of a landscape can even change overnight!

The soft earth of the plains is the easiest for a river to shape and mold. **Meanders** are the slow winding bends which a river takes through these flatter regions. As a river flows through the soft ground, it changes its course by eroding away the outer banks and depositing the sand and silt much farther downstream. Meanders can move very slowly down the plain this way, changing the landscape, and sometimes the borders between two countries.

Braided rivers are found in areas where lots of sediment is carried by the running water. The sediment is deposited in *bars* like long islands in the river bed and these often change position especially during times of flooding.

Ox-bow lakes are meander bends which have been cut off and left behind. A river can flow so fast during the spring floods that the land between the two bends is cut through. This leaves behind a lake with a special shape. It is called an "ox-bow" lake because it is shaped like the old-fashioned yoke used to harness oxen.

Running water is the most powerful kind of erosion which works on the landscape. There is another kind of "river" erosion that happens much more slowly. It is caused by rivers of ice which are called *glaciers.*

After many years this river has changed its path and has left behind an ox-bow lake and a wide strip of good farm land

Our Amazing World . . .

The Grand Canyon in the United States is a spectacular example of erosion. The land has been slowly pushed up at the same time as the Colorado River has worn it down. This double action has been going on for millions of years, carving beautiful shapes out of the earth. The canyon is over one mile deep in places, 4.5-15.5 miles wide and 235 miles long!

Glaciers

Glaciers are frozen rivers. Like rivers, glaciers also drain water off the land but they do it very slowly because the water is solid ice. Glaciers erode the land, but in a different way from rivers.

Glaciers are found in cold climates or high in the mountains where snow falls very deep in the winter. During the summer, there is not enough warmth to melt all of the snow. It slowly builds up year after year, like a giant frozen lake. When the snow becomes very deep, the bottom layers are crushed down to a solid piece of ice. Every year more snow is added to the pile until the tremendous weight of the packed snow makes the ice creep slowly down the slope.

Glaciers move down mountains like rivers in slow-motion. They are covered by winter snowfall, and melt away when their lower end reaches a warmer region. Glaciers move faster in warmer weather, sometimes as much as 65 feet a day. In winter time, they almost come to a full stop.

As a glacier moves down through the landscape, it acts like a huge piece of sandpaper. The glacier gathers up rocks, stones and earth from the land it crosses.

Inside a glacier, ice slowly cuts away at the rock and carries it down the mountain.

As this material is dragged along by the ice, it scrapes against the earth below. In this way, glaciers can make deep scratches in the rock. In time, glaciers can carve deep valleys out of the landscape. These valleys have a special U-shape which is different from the V-shaped valleys worn away by rivers.

As well as bringing snow down from high mountains, glaciers also drain the frozen water from very cold lands. Antarctica and Greenland are surrounded by many glaciers. They carry the built-up snow from the center out toward the sea.

When glaciers melt, they leave great piles of stones and earth littered on the ground. These piles are called *moraines.* Glaciers can also carve huge hollows out of the land. Water collects in these places making deep lakes. The Great Lakes in the northern United States were made by glaciers many millions of years ago.

Our Amazing World . . .

Since glaciers bring rocks, stones and silt down their slopes, there is no reason why they cannot carry anything else down the mountainside that gets trapped in their ice. There is a legend among mountain climbers that the body of a black spotted leopard lies frozen on the slopes of Mount Kilimanjaro in Tanzania. Perhaps it fell down an opening in the ice while out hunting. If the legend is true, one day the leopard's perfectly preserved, frozen body will reappear at the bottom of the glacier. Who knows what other surprises might be deep-frozen ready to be discovered in the future!

Lakes

Lakes are only a temporary part of the landscape. They are usually found where a river course has been blocked. When the water is backed up, a lake spreads out across the land. Lakes slowly change their shape and size as rivers fill them with sediment. To man they can be a valuable store of water and a useful source of power.

Lakes are hollows in the land often surrounded by higher ground. They can be made by glaciers, or caused by faults in the earth's crust. Sections of a river valley can be turned into lakes by landslides which block up the river's course. Lakes can also be made by man.

As well as the rain that falls on its surface, water also flows into a lake from the land around it. Rivers and streams from the surrounding drainage basin keep lakes full of water. This running water erodes sediment from the landscape and deposits it in the lake. These deposits can sometimes form into a delta. Water escapes from a lake by evaporating from the surface, seeping away underground or spilling over the edge to continue downstream. Some of the sediment is left

behind by the water, and the lake slowly begins to fill in. The lake is filled with more and more sediment over a period of many years. When it is finally filled in, the lake disappears. Its river has succeeded in smoothing over the hollow in the land and has evened out its path to the sea.

Some lakes are man-made. This is done by building a dam across a river. The dam makes the water rise to a much higher level. Water which is stored in the lake can be used for drinking or irrigation during the dry months of the year.

The force of the water can also be used to make electricity. When it is released from the dam, the weight of the falling water spins a giant turbine. The spinning turbine generates electricity which can be used by people living nearby. Sometimes a whole new city is built up around this plentiful supply of water and power. Boulder City, a town in Nevada, started this way.
The city grew up in the middle of the desert next to a dam built across the Colorado River. The lake made by the dam has created a lush green city where no one could live before.

Our Amazing World . . .

Lakes can appear wherever there is enough water to keep them filled. The highest lake in the world is Nam Tsho in the Himalayas. It is 15,180 feet above sea level. The Dead Sea in the Middle East is 1,286 feet below sea level. Lake Locharema in Northern Ireland vanishes underground in times of drought!

Index

Some entries in this index refer to pages in the other books of this series. They are as follows:

C	Continents and Climates	**W**	Weather
M	Mountains and Valleys	**R**	Rivers and Lakes
E	Earthquakes and Volcanoes	**S**	Seas and Oceans